M000201624

NAME

CONTACT INFORMATION

Unique

The Ultimate Planner for
Creative Professionals

ONE-EIGHTY
6-MONTH PLANNER

BroadStreet
PUBLISHING

BroadStreet Publishing Group LLC
Savage, Minnesota, USA
Broadstreetpublishing.com

Unique: *The Ultimate Planner for Creative Professionals*
© 2019 by Phil Cooke

ISBN 978-1-4245-5789-9

Design by Chris Garborg | garborgdesign.com
Editorial services by Michelle Winger | literallyprecise.com

Printed in China.

19 20 21 22 23 24 25   7 6 5 4 3 2 1

INTRODUCTION

The last thing creative professionals need are limits. That's why using productivity notebooks with too many pre-designed templates is frustrating. We don't need daily affirmations, motivation trackers, or rewards. We simply want the freedom to create. The *Unique: Ultimate Planner for Creative Professionals* is different. Our templates are simple—daily priorities, personal tasks, key calendar events, and plenty of space for other creative notes and wide-open thinking.

Why waste pages on monthly or weekly calendars when most of us share online calendars with our team? In a time when creative professionals are working with online productivity tools and apps for team communication, this unique planner is a key tool that brings today's priorities, tasks, and events together, so your creative thinking can be released.

If you're tired of wasting your day filling in mindless reports, meaningless templates, and information you'll never look at again, this planner is for you. Finally, a notebook that works for you instead of adding to your work.

Because creativity can't be forced; it can only be unleashed.

Phil Cook

MAJOR YEAR GOALS

- [ ]
- [ ]
- [ ]
- [ ]
- [ ]
- [ ]
- [ ]
- [ ]
- [ ]
- [ ]
- [ ]
- [ ]

HABITS TO DEVELOP

☐

☐

☐

☐

☐

☐

☐

☐

☐

☐

☐

☐

☐ BIG GOAL

NEXT STEPS
☐ _____
☐ _____
☐ _____

☐ BIG GOAL

NEXT STEPS
☐ _____
☐ _____
☐ _____

☐ BIG GOAL

NEXT STEPS
☐ _____
☐ _____
☐ _____

☐ BIG GOAL

NEXT STEPS
☐ _____
☐ _____
☐ _____

☐ BIG GOAL

NEXT STEPS
☐ _____
☐ _____
☐ _____

☐ BIG GOAL

NEXT STEPS
☐ _____
☐ _____
☐ _____

DATE

KEY CALENDAR EVENTS

PRIORITIES

☐ 1.

☐ 2.

☐ 3.

8

9

10

11

12

1

2

3

PERSONAL

☐

☐

☐

☐

☐

4

5

OTHER TASKS

☐

☐

☐

☐

☐

☐

☐

☐

Any proven tool that helps you see an objective view of your strengths and weaknesses is great. Without an adequate assessment, you'll never discover your true potential.

PHIL COOKE

DATE

KEY CALENDAR EVENTS

PRIORITIES

☐ 1.

☐ 2.

☐ 3.

8

9

10

11

12

1

2

3

4

5

PERSONAL

☐

☐

☐

☐

☐

OTHER TASKS

☐

☐

☐

☐

☐

☐

☐

☐

According to the grace of God given to me, like a skilled master builder I laid a foundation, and someone else is building upon it. Let each one take care how he builds upon it.

1 CORINTHIANS 3:10 ESV

DATE

KEY CALENDAR EVENTS

PRIORITIES

☐ 1.

☐ 2.

☐ 3.

8

9

10

11

12

1

2

3

4

5

PERSONAL

☐

☐

☐

☐

☐

OTHER TASKS

☐

☐

☐

☐

☐

☐

☐

10

Are you rationalizing second-best in your life? Have you been sucked into a regular paycheck or refuse to change because you're not willing to risk taking a hard look at your life, your gifts, and your future?

PHIL COOKE

11

DATE

PRIORITIES

☐ 1.

☐ 2.

☐ 3.

PERSONAL

☐

☐

☐

☐

☐

KEY CALENDAR EVENTS

8

9

10

11

12

1

2

3

4

5

OTHER TASKS

☐

☐

☐

☐

☐

☐

☐

☐

A leader takes people where they want to go. A great leader takes people where they don't necessarily want to go, but ought to be.

ROSALYNN CARTER

DATE

KEY CALENDAR EVENTS

PRIORITIES

- [ ] 1.
- [ ] 2.
- [ ] 3.

8

9

10

11

12

1

2

3

4

5

PERSONAL

- [ ]
- [ ]
- [ ]
- [ ]
- [ ]

OTHER TASKS

- [ ]
- [ ]
- [ ]
- [ ]
- [ ]
- [ ]
- [ ]
- [ ]

A significant part of being different is being honest about who you are and how you're perceived.
PHIL COOKE

15

DATE
_____

KEY CALENDAR EVENTS
_____
_____

PRIORITIES

☐ 1. _____
_____

☐ 2. _____
_____

☐ 3. _____
_____

8 _____
9 _____
10 _____
11 _____
12 _____
1 _____
2 _____
3 _____
4 _____
5 _____
_____
_____

PERSONAL

☐ _____
☐ _____
☐ _____
☐ _____
☐ _____

OTHER TASKS

☐ --
☐ --
☐ --
☐ --
☐ --
☐ --
☐ --
☐ --

Curiosity about life in all of its aspects, I think, is still the secret of great creative people.

LEO BURNETT

DATE

KEY CALENDAR EVENTS

PRIORITIES

☐ 1.

☐ 2.

☐ 3.

8

9

10

11

12

1

2

3

4

5

PERSONAL

☐

☐

☐

☐

☐

OTHER TASKS

☐

☐

☐

☐

☐

☐

☐

☐

Anything that hinders or frustrates the full operation of your gifts and talents is something that should be dealt with as soon as possible.

PHIL COOKE

19

DATE

KEY CALENDAR EVENTS

PRIORITIES

☐ 1.

☐ 2.

☐ 3.

8

9

10

11

12

1

2

3

PERSONAL

☐

☐

☐

☐

☐

4

5

OTHER TASKS

☐

☐

☐

☐

☐

☐

☐

☐

20

Art enables us to find ourselves and lose ourselves at the same time.

THOMAS MERTON

21

DATE

KEY CALENDAR EVENTS

PRIORITIES

1.

2.

3.

8

9

10

11

12

1

2

3

4

5

PERSONAL

OTHER TASKS

As you gain expertise and credibility in an area you're extraordinarily passionate about, you'll immediately begin to influence the people around you. It's tough not to notice a raging fire.

PHIL COOKE

23

DATE

PRIORITIES

☐ 1.

☐ 2.

☐ 3.

PERSONAL

☐

☐

☐

☐

☐

KEY CALENDAR EVENTS

8

9

10

11

12

1

2

3

4

5

OTHER TASKS

☐

☐

☐

☐

☐

☐

☐

☐

Be yourself; everyone else is already taken.
OSCAR WILDE

25

DATE

KEY CALENDAR EVENTS

PRIORITIES

☐ 1.

☐ 2.

☐ 3.

8

9

10

11

12

1

2

3

4

5

PERSONAL

☐

☐

☐

☐

☐

OTHER TASKS

☐

☐

☐

☐

☐

☐

☐

☐

26

Being truthful about what distinguishes you from the pack is a critical step in finding your identity and ultimately your future.

PHIL COOKE

DATE

KEY CALENDAR EVENTS

PRIORITIES

☐ 1.

☐ 2.

☐ 3.

8

9

10

11

12

1

2

3

4

5

PERSONAL

☐

☐

☐

☐

☐

OTHER TASKS

☐

☐

☐

☐

☐

☐

☐

☐

"Nothing will be impossible with God."

LUKE 1:37 ESV

29

DATE

KEY CALENDAR EVENTS

PRIORITIES

☐ 1.

☐ 2.

☐ 3.

8

9

10

11

12

1

2

3

4

5

PERSONAL

☐

☐

☐

☐

☐

OTHER TASKS

☐

☐

☐

☐

☐

☐

☐

☐

30

Being truthful and responsible can add to your reputation— even during periods of desperate challenge.
PHIL COOKE

31

DATE

KEY CALENDAR EVENTS

PRIORITIES

- [ ] 1.
- [ ] 2.
- [ ] 3.

8

9

10

11

12

1

2

3

4

5

PERSONAL

- [ ]
- [ ]
- [ ]
- [ ]
- [ ]

OTHER TASKS

- [ ]
- [ ]
- [ ]
- [ ]
- [ ]
- [ ]
- [ ]
- [ ]

Creativity is contagious; pass it on.
ALBERT EINSTEIN

DATE

KEY CALENDAR EVENTS

PRIORITIES

☐ 1.

☐ 2.

☐ 3.

8

9

10

11

12

1

2

3

PERSONAL

☐

☐

☐

☐

☐

4

5

OTHER TASKS

☐

☐

☐

☐

☐

☐

☐

☐

Clarity is a sign of
intellectual energy.
PHIL COOKE

35

DATE

PRIORITIES

- [ ] 1.
- [ ] 2.
- [ ] 3.

PERSONAL

- [ ]
- [ ]
- [ ]
- [ ]
- [ ]

KEY CALENDAR EVENTS

8

9

10

11

12

1

2

3

4

5

OTHER TASKS

- [ ]
- [ ]
- [ ]
- [ ]
- [ ]
- [ ]
- [ ]
- [ ]

Do not neglect your gift.
1 TIMOTHY 4:14 NIV

37

DATE

KEY CALENDAR EVENTS

PRIORITIES

☐ 1.

☐ 2.

☐ 3.

8

9

10

11

12

1

2

3

PERSONAL

☐

☐

☐

☐

☐

4

5

OTHER TASKS

☐

☐

☐

☐

☐

☐

☐

☐

Do you believe in your purpose and calling enough to step up to the plate and swing for the fence?

PHIL COOKE

DATE

KEY CALENDAR EVENTS

PRIORITIES

- [ ] 1.
- [ ] 2.
- [ ] 3.

8

9

10

11

12

1

2

3

4

5

PERSONAL

- [ ]
- [ ]
- [ ]
- [ ]
- [ ]

OTHER TASKS

- [ ]
- [ ]
- [ ]
- [ ]
- [ ]
- [ ]
- [ ]

Do you know yourself and your purpose well enough to be ready when your moment of destiny arrives?

PHIL COOKE

41

DATE

KEY CALENDAR EVENTS

PRIORITIES

☐ 1.

☐ 2.

☐ 3.

8

9

10

11

12

1

2

3

PERSONAL

☐

☐

☐

☐

☐

4

5

OTHER TASKS

☐

☐

☐

☐

☐

☐

☐

☐

Daring ideas are like chessmen moved forward; they may be beaten, but they may start a winning game.

GOETHE

43

DATE

KEY CALENDAR EVENTS

PRIORITIES

☐ 1.

☐ 2.

☐ 3.

8

9

10

11

12

1

2

3

4

5

PERSONAL

☐

☐

☐

☐

☐

OTHER TASKS

☐

☐

☐

☐

☐

☐

☐

☐

Don't live out other people's dreams and refuse to act on who you were created to be.

PHIL COOKE

45

DATE

KEY CALENDAR EVENTS

PRIORITIES

- [ ] 1.
- [ ] 2.
- [ ] 3.

8

9

10

11

12

1

2

3

4

5

PERSONAL

- [ ]
- [ ]
- [ ]
- [ ]
- [ ]

OTHER TASKS

- [ ]
- [ ]
- [ ]
- [ ]
- [ ]
- [ ]
- [ ]
- [ ]

Delete the negative;
accentuate the positive.
DONNA KARAN

47

DATE

KEY CALENDAR EVENTS

PRIORITIES

☐ 1.

☐ 2.

☐ 3.

8

9

10

11

12

1

2

3

4

5

PERSONAL

☐

☐

☐

☐

☐

OTHER TASKS

☐

☐

☐

☐

☐

☐

☐

☐

Don't write because you have all the answers; write because you have lots of questions.

PHIL COOKE

DATE

KEY CALENDAR EVENTS

PRIORITIES

1.

2.

3.

8

9

10

11

12

1

2

3

PERSONAL

4

5

OTHER TASKS

Done is better than perfect.

SHERYL SANDBERG

51

DATE

KEY CALENDAR EVENTS

PRIORITIES

- [ ] 1.
- [ ] 2.
- [ ] 3.

8
9
10
11
12
1
2
3
4
5

PERSONAL

- [ ]
- [ ]
- [ ]
- [ ]
- [ ]

OTHER TASKS

- [ ]
- [ ]
- [ ]
- [ ]
- [ ]
- [ ]
- [ ]
- [ ]

Are you taking the easy way out?
You can't sit on the sofa and wait
for God when you should be
learning, growing, and developing
your gifts and talents.
PHIL COOKE

DATE

KEY CALENDAR EVENTS

PRIORITIES

☐ 1.

☐ 2.

☐ 3.

8

9

10

11

12

1

2

3

4

5

PERSONAL

☐

☐

☐

☐

☐

OTHER TASKS

☐

☐

☐

☐

☐

☐

☐

☐

Each of you should use whatever gift you have received to serve others, as faithful stewards of God's grace in its various forms.

1 PETER 4:10 NIV

DATE

KEY CALENDAR EVENTS

PRIORITIES

☐ 1.

☐ 2.

☐ 3.

8

9

10

11

12

1

2

3

4

5

PERSONAL

☐

☐

☐

☐

☐

OTHER TASKS

☐

☐

☐

☐

☐

☐

☐

☐

Each person must live their life as a model for others.

ROSA PARKS

57

DATE

KEY CALENDAR EVENTS

PRIORITIES

☐ 1.

☐ 2.

☐ 3.

8

9

10

11

12

1

2

3

PERSONAL

☐

☐

☐

☐

☐

4

5

OTHER TASKS

☐

☐

☐

☐

☐

☐

☐

☐

Education was my father's way out of poverty. He taught me that learning was incredibly valuable.

PHIL COOKE

DATE

KEY CALENDAR EVENTS

PRIORITIES

- [ ] 1.
- [ ] 2.
- [ ] 3.

8

9

10

11

12

1

2

3

4

5

PERSONAL

- [ ]
- [ ]
- [ ]
- [ ]
- [ ]

OTHER TASKS

- [ ]
- [ ]
- [ ]
- [ ]
- [ ]
- [ ]
- [ ]
- [ ]

Think left and think right
and think low and think high.
Oh, the thinks you can think
up if only you try.
DR. SEUSS

DATE

KEY CALENDAR EVENTS

PRIORITIES

☐ 1. _____

☐ 2. _____

☐ 3. _____

8 _____

9 _____

10 _____

11 _____

12 _____

1 _____

2 _____

3 _____

4 _____

5 _____

PERSONAL

☐ _____

☐ _____

☐ _____

☐ _____

☐ _____

OTHER TASKS

☐ --

☐ --

☐ --

☐ --

☐ --

☐ --

☐ --

☐ --

People don't pay for average; they pay for great.
PHIL COOKE

63

DATE

KEY CALENDAR EVENTS

PRIORITIES

- [ ] 1.
- [ ] 2.
- [ ] 3.

8

9

10

11

12

1

2

3

4

5

PERSONAL

- [ ]
- [ ]
- [ ]
- [ ]
- [ ]

OTHER TASKS

- [ ]
- [ ]
- [ ]
- [ ]
- [ ]
- [ ]
- [ ]
- [ ]

God chose to introduce Himself to us in the first verse of Genesis as a Creator. And yet so few people really understand the power of creativity to influence the culture.

PHIL COOKE

DATE

KEY CALENDAR EVENTS

PRIORITIES

☐ 1.

☐ 2.

☐ 3.

8
9
10
11
12
1
2
3
4
5

PERSONAL

☐
☐
☐
☐
☐

OTHER TASKS

☐
☐
☐
☐
☐
☐
☐
☐

66

I praise you, for I am fearfully
and wonderfully made.
Wonderful are your works;
my soul knows it very well.

PSALM 139:14 ESV

DATE

KEY CALENDAR EVENTS

PRIORITIES

☐ 1.

☐ 2.

☐ 3.

8

9

10

11

12

1

2

3

4

5

PERSONAL

☐

☐

☐

☐

☐

OTHER TASKS

☐

☐

☐

☐

☐

☐

☐

☐

68

God gave you a unique DNA. Your job is to discover how your unique gifts and talents can differentiate you from everyone else.

PHIL COOKE

DATE

KEY CALENDAR EVENTS

PRIORITIES

☐ 1.

☐ 2.

☐ 3.

8

9

10

11

12

1

2

3

4

5

PERSONAL

☐

☐

☐

☐

☐

OTHER TASKS

☐

☐

☐

☐

☐

☐

☐

Greater than the tread of mighty armies is an idea whose time has come.

VICTOR HUGO

71

DATE

KEY CALENDAR EVENTS

PRIORITIES

☐ 1.

☐ 2.

☐ 3.

8

9

10

11

12

1

2

3

PERSONAL

☐

☐

☐

☐

☐

4

5

OTHER TASKS

☐

☐

☐

☐

☐

☐

☐

☐

72

Half the battle of getting things done is just getting them down. Write them down.

PHIL COOKE

DATE

KEY CALENDAR EVENTS

PRIORITIES

- [ ] 1.
- [ ] 2.
- [ ] 3.

8
9
10
11
12
1
2
3
4
5

PERSONAL

- [ ]
- [ ]
- [ ]
- [ ]
- [ ]

OTHER TASKS

- [ ]
- [ ]
- [ ]
- [ ]
- [ ]
- [ ]
- [ ]
- [ ]

I'm convinced that about half of what separates the successful entrepreneurs from the non-successful ones is pure perseverance.
STEVE JOBS

75

DATE

KEY CALENDAR EVENTS

PRIORITIES

- [ ] 1. _____
  _____
- [ ] 2. _____
  _____
- [ ] 3. _____
  _____

8 _____
9 _____
10 _____
11 _____
12 _____
1 _____
2 _____
3 _____
4 _____
5 _____
_____
_____

PERSONAL

- [ ] _____
- [ ] _____
- [ ] _____
- [ ] _____
- [ ] _____

OTHER TASKS

- [ ] --
- [ ] --
- [ ] --
- [ ] --
- [ ] --
- [ ] --
- [ ] --
- [ ] --

Having an accurate understanding of what makes you unique and different is absolutely critical.

PHIL COOKE

DATE

KEY CALENDAR EVENTS

PRIORITIES

- [ ] 1.
- [ ] 2.
- [ ] 3.

8
9
10
11
12
1
2
3
4
5

PERSONAL

- [ ]
- [ ]
- [ ]
- [ ]
- [ ]

OTHER TASKS

- [ ]
- [ ]
- [ ]
- [ ]
- [ ]
- [ ]
- [ ]
- [ ]

Honesty guides good people;
dishonesty destroys
treacherous people.
PROVERBS 11:3 NLT

DATE

KEY CALENDAR EVENTS

PRIORITIES

☐ 1.

☐ 2.

☐ 3.

8

9

10

11

12

1

2

3

4

5

PERSONAL

☐

☐

☐

☐

☐

OTHER TASKS

☐

☐

☐

☐

☐

☐

☐

☐

How much time do you
spend talking when you
should be doing?
PHIL COOKE

81

DATE

KEY CALENDAR EVENTS

PRIORITIES

☐ 1.

☐ 2.

☐ 3.

8

9

10

11

12

1

2

3

4

5

PERSONAL

☐

☐

☐

☐

☐

OTHER TASKS

☐

☐

☐

☐

☐

☐

☐

☐

I never dreamed about
success. I worked for it.
ESTÉE LAUDER

DATE

KEY CALENDAR EVENTS

PRIORITIES

☐ 1.

☐ 2.

☐ 3.

8

9

10

11

12

1

2

3

4

5

PERSONAL

☐

☐

☐

☐

☐

OTHER TASKS

☐

☐

☐

☐

☐

☐

☐

☐

Ideas are powerful, and stories are ideas in action.
PHIL COOKE

DATE

KEY CALENDAR EVENTS

PRIORITIES

- [ ] 1.
- [ ] 2.
- [ ] 3.

8

9

10

11

12

1

2

3

4

5

PERSONAL

- [ ]
- [ ]
- [ ]
- [ ]
- [ ]

OTHER TASKS

- [ ]
- [ ]
- [ ]
- [ ]
- [ ]
- [ ]
- [ ]
- [ ]

86

Ideas are the most fragile things in the world, and if you do not write them down, they could be lost forever.

PHIL COOKE

DATE

KEY CALENDAR EVENTS

PRIORITIES

☐ 1.

☐ 2.

☐ 3.

8

9

10

11

12

1

2

3

PERSONAL

☐

☐

☐

☐

☐

4

5

OTHER TASKS

☐

☐

☐

☐

☐

☐

☐

☐

88

If you hear a voice within you say, "You cannot paint," then by all means paint, and that voice will be silenced.

VINCENT VAN GOGH

DATE
_____

KEY CALENDAR EVENTS

_____

_____

PRIORITIES

☐ 1. _____

_____

☐ 2. _____

_____

☐ 3. _____

_____

8 _____

9 _____

10 _____

11 _____

12 _____

1 _____

2 _____

3 _____

4 _____

5 _____

_____

_____

PERSONAL

☐ _____

☐ _____

☐ _____

☐ _____

☐ _____

OTHER TASKS

☐ --

☐ --

☐ --

☐ --

☐ --

☐ --

☐ --

☐ --

90

If you want to achieve greatness, stop asking for permission.

PHIL COOKE

91

DATE

KEY CALENDAR EVENTS

PRIORITIES

☐ 1.

☐ 2.

☐ 3.

8

9

10

11

12

1

2

3

4

5

PERSONAL

☐

☐

☐

☐

☐

OTHER TASKS

☐

☐

☐

☐

☐

☐

☐

☐

Do you see a man skillful in his work?
He will stand before kings; he will not
stand before obscure men.

PROVERBS 22:29 ESV

DATE

KEY CALENDAR EVENTS

PRIORITIES

☐ 1.

☐ 2.

☐ 3.

8

9

10

11

12

1

2

3

4

5

PERSONAL

☐

☐

☐

☐

☐

OTHER TASKS

☐

☐

☐

☐

☐

☐

☐

☐

94

If your actions create a legacy that inspires others to dream more, learn more, do more, and become more, then you are an excellent leader.

DOLLY PARTON

DATE

KEY CALENDAR EVENTS

PRIORITIES

- [ ] 1.
- [ ] 2.
- [ ] 3.

8
9
10
11
12
1
2
3
4
5

PERSONAL

- [ ]
- [ ]
- [ ]
- [ ]
- [ ]

OTHER TASKS

- [ ]
- [ ]
- [ ]
- [ ]
- [ ]
- [ ]
- [ ]
- [ ]

People follow visionaries—especially those who know what they're talking about.

PHIL COOKE

97

DATE

KEY CALENDAR EVENTS

PRIORITIES

☐ 1.

☐ 2.

☐ 3.

8

9

10

11

12

1

2

3

4

5

PERSONAL

☐

☐

☐

☐

☐

OTHER TASKS

☐

☐

☐

☐

☐

☐

☐

☐

98

Invite people into your life that don't look or think like you.

MELLODY HOBSON

DATE

KEY CALENDAR EVENTS

PRIORITIES

1.

2.

3.

8

9

10

11

12

1

2

3

PERSONAL

4

5

OTHER TASKS

It doesn't matter if you have a great message if no one is listening.
PHIL COOKE

101

DATE

KEY CALENDAR EVENTS

PRIORITIES

☐ 1.

☐ 2.

☐ 3.

8

9

10

11

12

1

2

3

4

5

PERSONAL

☐

☐

☐

☐

☐

OTHER TASKS

☐

☐

☐

☐

☐

☐

☐

Creativity is intelligence having fun.
ALBERT EINSTEIN

DATE

KEY CALENDAR EVENTS

PRIORITIES

1.

2.

3.

8

9

10

11

12

1

2

3

4

5

PERSONAL

OTHER TASKS

It's time to stop looking for the biggest crowd and start looking for the right crowd.
PHIL COOKE

DATE

KEY CALENDAR EVENTS

PRIORITIES

☐ 1.

☐ 2.

☐ 3.

8

9

10

11

12

1

2

3

4

5

PERSONAL

☐

☐

☐

☐

☐

OTHER TASKS

☐

☐

☐

☐

☐

☐

☐

☐

Keep your heart with all vigilance, for from it flow the springs of life.
PROVERBS 4:23 ESV

DATE

KEY CALENDAR EVENTS

PRIORITIES

☐ 1.

☐ 2.

☐ 3.

8

9

10

11

12

1

2

3

4

5

PERSONAL

☐

☐

☐

☐

☐

OTHER TASKS

☐

☐

☐

☐

☐

☐

☐

☐

Knowing what matters—
what you value—is key
to living a life of meaning
and purpose.
PHIL COOKE

DATE

KEY CALENDAR EVENTS

PRIORITIES

1.

2.

3.

8

9

10

11

12

1

2

3

4

5

PERSONAL

OTHER TASKS

If competition from others is making it more difficult to get noticed, then perhaps you should consider a different niche.

PHIL COOKE

DATE

KEY CALENDAR EVENTS

PRIORITIES

☐ 1.

☐ 2.

☐ 3.

8

9

10

11

12

1

2

3

4

5

PERSONAL

☐

☐

☐

☐

☐

OTHER TASKS

☐

☐

☐

☐

☐

☐

☐

☐

Education without values, as useful as it is, seems rather to make man a more clever devil.

C.S. LEWIS

113

DATE

KEY CALENDAR EVENTS

PRIORITIES

- 1.
- 2.
- 3.

8

9

10

11

12

1

2

3

4

5

PERSONAL

OTHER TASKS

Learn to take what most people consider a negative and turn it into a positive.
PHIL COOKE

DATE

KEY CALENDAR EVENTS

PRIORITIES

- [ ] 1.
- [ ] 2.
- [ ] 3.

8
9
10
11
12
1
2
3
4
5

PERSONAL

- [ ]
- [ ]
- [ ]
- [ ]
- [ ]

OTHER TASKS

- [ ]
- [ ]
- [ ]
- [ ]
- [ ]
- [ ]
- [ ]
- [ ]

We must remember that failure gives us chances to grow, and we ignore those chances at our own peril.

ED CATMULL

DATE

PRIORITIES

☐ 1.

☐ 2.

☐ 3.

PERSONAL

☐

☐

☐

☐

☐

KEY CALENDAR EVENTS

8

9

10

11

12

1

2

3

4

5

OTHER TASKS

☐

☐

☐

☐

☐

☐

☐

☐

Learn to work within your limitations—or better yet—use them to your advantage.
PHIL COOKE

DATE

KEY CALENDAR EVENTS

PRIORITIES

☐ 1.

☐ 2.

☐ 3.

8

9

10

11

12

1

2

3

PERSONAL

☐

☐

☐

☐

☐

4

5

OTHER TASKS

☐

☐

☐

☐

☐

☐

☐

☐

Life is either a daring adventure or nothing at all.

HELEN KELLER

121

DATE

KEY CALENDAR EVENTS

PRIORITIES

☐ 1.

☐ 2.

☐ 3.

8

9

10

11

12

1

2

3

4

5

PERSONAL

☐

☐

☐

☐

☐

OTHER TASKS

☐

☐

☐

☐

☐

☐

☐

☐

122

Your influence begins with discovering what you were born to accomplish.
PHIL COOKE

123

DATE

KEY CALENDAR EVENTS

PRIORITIES

☐ 1.

☐ 2.

☐ 3.

8

9

10

11

12

1

2

3

PERSONAL

☐

☐

☐

☐

☐

4

5

OTHER TASKS

☐

☐

☐

☐

☐

☐

☐

☐

124

Logic will get you from A to B. Imagination will take you everywhere.

DATE

KEY CALENDAR EVENTS

PRIORITIES

☐ 1.

☐ 2.

☐ 3.

8

9

10

11

12

1

2

3

4

5

PERSONAL

☐

☐

☐

☐

☐

OTHER TASKS

☐

☐

☐

☐

☐

☐

☐

☐

126

Love your friends and respect them. But never abandon your dream because your friends lack the vision to join you.

PHIL COOKE

DATE

KEY CALENDAR EVENTS

PRIORITIES

1.

2.

3.

8

9

10

11

12

1

2

3

4

5

PERSONAL

OTHER TASKS

Never give up, for that is just the place and time that the tide will turn.

HARRIET BEECHER STOWE

129

DATE

KEY CALENDAR EVENTS

PRIORITIES

☐ 1.

☐ 2.

☐ 3.

8

9

10

11

12

1

2

3

PERSONAL

☐

☐

☐

☐

☐

4

5

OTHER TASKS

☐

☐

☐

☐

☐

☐

☐

☐

130

Most unsuccessful people are unsuccessful because they either can't or won't decide on the important priorities in their lives.

PHIL COOKE

DATE

KEY CALENDAR EVENTS

PRIORITIES

☐ 1.

☐ 2.

☐ 3.

8

9

10

11

12

1

2

3

4

5

PERSONAL

☐

☐

☐

☐

☐

OTHER TASKS

☐

☐

☐

☐

☐

☐

☐

Lazy people don't even cook
the game they catch,
but the diligent make use
of everything they find.
PROVERBS 12:27 NLT

DATE

KEY CALENDAR EVENTS

PRIORITIES

1.

2.

3.

8

9

10

11

12

1

2

3

4

5

PERSONAL

OTHER TASKS

Never close the door on the possibilities God can accomplish through your life with or without the appropriate skill set.
PHIL COOKE

135

DATE

KEY CALENDAR EVENTS

PRIORITIES

☐ 1.

☐ 2.

☐ 3.

8

9

10

11

12

1

2

3

PERSONAL

☐

☐

☐

☐

☐

4

5

OTHER TASKS

☐ --

☐ --

☐ --

☐ --

☐ --

☐ --

☐ --

☐ --

No amount of ability is of the slightest avail without honor.

ANDREW CARNEGIE

137

DATE

KEY CALENDAR EVENTS

PRIORITIES

☐ 1.

☐ 2.

☐ 3.

8

9

10

11

12

1

2

3

4

5

PERSONAL

☐

☐

☐

☐

☐

OTHER TASKS

☐

☐

☐

☐

☐

☐

☐

☐

One reason stories work is because we want to experience the emotions, feelings, and passions of others who have encountered the challenges we face each day.

PHIL COOKE

DATE

PRIORITIES

☐ 1. _____

_____

☐ 2. _____

_____

☐ 3. _____

_____

PERSONAL

☐ _____

☐ _____

☐ _____

☐ _____

☐ _____

KEY CALENDAR EVENTS

_____

_____

8 _____

9 _____

10 _____

11 _____

12 _____

1 _____

2 _____

3 _____

4 _____

5 _____

_____

_____

OTHER TASKS

☐ ---

☐ ---

☐ ---

☐ ---

☐ ---

☐ ---

☐ ---

☐ ---

Passion is one of the most contagious emotions on the planet, and people will line up to follow it, especially when the passionate person has credibility.

PHIL COOKE

DATE

KEY CALENDAR EVENTS

PRIORITIES

- [ ] 1.
- [ ] 2.
- [ ] 3.

8
9
10
11
12
1
2
3
4
5

PERSONAL

- [ ]
- [ ]
- [ ]
- [ ]
- [ ]

OTHER TASKS

- [ ]
- [ ]
- [ ]
- [ ]
- [ ]
- [ ]
- [ ]
- [ ]

Reason can answer questions, but imagination has to ask them.
RALPH GERARD

DATE

KEY CALENDAR EVENTS

PRIORITIES

☐ 1.

☐ 2.

☐ 3.

8

9

10

11

12

1

2

3

4

5

PERSONAL

☐

☐

☐

☐

☐

OTHER TASKS

☐

☐

☐

☐

☐

☐

☐

☐

In an age of skepticism and media diversification, people need to easily understand who you are and how to relate to your idea or dream. Otherwise, you'll be lost in the sea of alternatives.

PHIL COOKE

DATE

KEY CALENDAR EVENTS

PRIORITIES

☐ 1.

☐ 2.

☐ 3.

8

9

10

11

12

1

2

3

4

5

PERSONAL

☐

☐

☐

☐

☐

OTHER TASKS

☐

☐

☐

☐

☐

☐

☐

☐

146

Finding your honest voice in the middle of the madness is critical.
PHIL COOKE

DATE

KEY CALENDAR EVENTS

PRIORITIES

☐ 1.

☐ 2.

☐ 3.

8

9

10

11

12

1

2

3

4

5

PERSONAL

☐

☐

☐

☐

☐

OTHER TASKS

☐

☐

☐

☐

☐

☐

☐

☐

People will forget what you said, and people will forget what you did, but people will never forget how you made them feel.

MAYA ANGELOU

DATE

KEY CALENDAR EVENTS

PRIORITIES

☐ 1.

☐ 2.

☐ 3.

8

9

10

11

12

1

2

3

4

5

PERSONAL

☐

☐

☐

☐

☐

OTHER TASKS

☐

☐

☐

☐

☐

☐

☐

Values are the bumpers on the bowling alley of life. They determine our boundaries—how far we'll go on questionable issues.

PHIL COOKE

DATE

KEY CALENDAR EVENTS

PRIORITIES

☐ 1.

☐ 2.

☐ 3.

8

9

10

11

12

1

2

3

4

5

PERSONAL

☐

☐

☐

☐

☐

OTHER TASKS

☐

☐

☐

☐

☐

☐

☐

☐

The Spirit God gave us does not make us timid, but gives us power, love and self-discipline.

2 TIMOTHY 1:7 NIV

DATE

KEY CALENDAR EVENTS

PRIORITIES

☐ 1.

☐ 2.

☐ 3.

8

9

10

11

12

1

2

3

4

5

PERSONAL

☐

☐

☐

☐

☐

OTHER TASKS

☐

☐

☐

☐

☐

☐

☐

☐

Some choices are better than others. Some decisions make sense and others don't. Values matter.

PHIL COOKE

DATE

KEY CALENDAR EVENTS

PRIORITIES

- [ ] 1.
- [ ] 2.
- [ ] 3.

8
9
10
11
12
1
2
3
4
5

PERSONAL

- [ ]
- [ ]
- [ ]
- [ ]
- [ ]

OTHER TASKS

- [ ]
- [ ]
- [ ]
- [ ]
- [ ]
- [ ]
- [ ]
- [ ]

Start asking the
right questions.
PHIL COOKE

DATE

KEY CALENDAR EVENTS

PRIORITIES

☐ 1.

☐ 2.

☐ 3.

8

9

10

11

12

1

2

3

4

5

PERSONAL

☐

☐

☐

☐

☐

OTHER TASKS

☐

☐

☐

☐

☐

☐

☐

☐

The most effective way to do it is to do it.
AMELIA EARHART

DATE

KEY CALENDAR EVENTS

PRIORITIES

☐ 1.

☐ 2.

☐ 3.

8

9

10

11

12

1

2

3

4

5

PERSONAL

☐

☐

☐

☐

☐

OTHER TASKS

☐

☐

☐

☐

☐

☐

☐

☐

Stop taking charge and start taking responsibility.

PHIL COOKE

DATE

KEY CALENDAR EVENTS

PRIORITIES

☐ 1.

☐ 2.

☐ 3.

8

9

10

11

12

1

2

3

4

5

PERSONAL

☐

☐

☐

☐

☐

OTHER TASKS

☐

☐

☐

☐

☐

☐

☐

☐

Success isn't a short game.
PHIL COOKE

163

DATE

KEY CALENDAR EVENTS

PRIORITIES

☐ 1.

☐ 2.

☐ 3.

8

9

10

11

12

1

2

3

4

5

PERSONAL

☐

☐

☐

☐

☐

OTHER TASKS

☐

☐

☐

☐

☐

☐

☐

☐

The difference between successful people and others is how long they spend feeling sorry for themselves.
BARBARA CORCORAN

165

DATE

KEY CALENDAR EVENTS

PRIORITIES

- [ ] 1.
- [ ] 2.
- [ ] 3.

8
9
10
11
12
1
2
3
4
5

PERSONAL

- [ ]
- [ ]
- [ ]
- [ ]
- [ ]

OTHER TASKS

- [ ]
- [ ]
- [ ]
- [ ]
- [ ]
- [ ]
- [ ]
- [ ]

The most creative approach is often the simple approach.

PHIL COOKE

DATE

KEY CALENDAR EVENTS

PRIORITIES

☐ 1.

☐ 2.

☐ 3.

8

9

10

11

12

1

2

3

4

5

PERSONAL

☐

☐

☐

☐

☐

OTHER TASKS

☐

☐

☐

☐

☐

☐

☐

☐

Whatever you do, work heartily,
as for the Lord and not for men,
knowing that from the Lord you will
receive the inheritance as your reward.
COLOSSIANS 3:23-24 ESV

DATE

KEY CALENDAR EVENTS

PRIORITIES

☐ 1.

☐ 2.

☐ 3.

8

9

10

11

12

1

2

3

4

5

PERSONAL

☐

☐

☐

☐

☐

OTHER TASKS

☐

☐

☐

☐

☐

☐

☐

☐

The most valuable commodity of the 21st century will be undivided attention.

PHIL COOKE

DATE

PRIORITIES

- [ ] 1.
- [ ] 2.
- [ ] 3.

PERSONAL

- [ ]
- [ ]
- [ ]
- [ ]
- [ ]

KEY CALENDAR EVENTS

8
9
10
11
12
1
2
3
4
5

OTHER TASKS

- [ ]
- [ ]
- [ ]
- [ ]
- [ ]
- [ ]
- [ ]
- [ ]

The old saying is true: your daily decisions determine your destiny.
PHIL COOKE

DATE

KEY CALENDAR EVENTS

PRIORITIES

- [ ] 1.
- [ ] 2.
- [ ] 3.

8

9

10

11

12

1

2

3

4

5

PERSONAL

- [ ]
- [ ]
- [ ]
- [ ]
- [ ]

OTHER TASKS

- [ ]
- [ ]
- [ ]
- [ ]
- [ ]
- [ ]
- [ ]
- [ ]

The principle of true art is not to portray, but to evoke.

JERZY KOSINSKI

DATE

KEY CALENDAR EVENTS

PRIORITIES

☐ 1.

☐ 2.

☐ 3.

8

9

10

11

12

1

2

3

4

5

PERSONAL

☐

☐

☐

☐

☐

OTHER TASKS

☐

☐

☐

☐

☐

☐

☐

☐

The question isn't "What do you do?" or "How do you do it?" The real question is "Who are you?"

PHIL COOKE

177

DATE

KEY CALENDAR EVENTS

PRIORITIES

☐ 1.

☐ 2.

☐ 3.

8

9

10

11

12

1

2

PERSONAL

☐

☐

☐

☐

☐

3

4

5

OTHER TASKS

☐

☐

☐

☐

☐

☐

☐

☐

Your ability to influence the next generation is tied to knowing and understanding your single-minded purpose.

PHIL COOKE

DATE

KEY CALENDAR EVENTS

PRIORITIES

☐ 1.

☐ 2.

☐ 3.

8

9

10

11

12

1

2

3

4

5

PERSONAL

☐

☐

☐

☐

☐

OTHER TASKS

☐

☐

☐

☐

☐

☐

☐

☐

The wisdom that is from above is first pure, then peaceable, gentle, and easy to be intreated, full of mercy and good fruits, without partiality, and without hypocrisy.

JAMES 3:17 KJV

DATE

KEY CALENDAR EVENTS

PRIORITIES

☐ 1.

☐ 2.

☐ 3.

8

9

10

11

12

1

2

3

PERSONAL

☐

☐

☐

☐

☐

4

5

OTHER TASKS

☐

☐

☐

☐

☐

☐

☐

☐

The world isn't looking for a copy of an existing writer, musician, politician, CEO, or leader; they're looking for someone new, innovative, and original.

PHIL COOKE

DATE

KEY CALENDAR EVENTS

PRIORITIES

☐ 1.

☐ 2.

☐ 3.

8

9

10

11

12

1

2

3

4

5

PERSONAL

☐

☐

☐

☐

☐

OTHER TASKS

☐

☐

☐

☐

☐

☐

☐

☐

We are not interested in
the possibilities of defeat.
They do not exist.
QUEEN VICTORIA

185

DATE

KEY CALENDAR EVENTS

PRIORITIES

☐ 1.

☐ 2.

☐ 3.

8

9

10

11

12

1

2

3

4

5

PERSONAL

☐

☐

☐

☐

☐

OTHER TASKS

☐

☐

☐

☐

☐

☐

☐

☐

There are few things in life more satisfying than seeing lives changed on a global scale.

PHIL COOKE

DATE

KEY CALENDAR EVENTS

PRIORITIES

☐ 1.

☐ 2.

☐ 3.

PERSONAL

☐
☐
☐
☐
☐

8

9

10

11

12

1

2

3

4

5

OTHER TASKS

☐
☐
☐
☐
☐
☐
☐
☐

There's no substitute for real experience and accomplishment.
PHIL COOKE

DATE

KEY CALENDAR EVENTS

PRIORITIES

☐ 1.

☐ 2.

☐ 3.

8

9

10

11

12

1

2

3

4

5

PERSONAL

☐

☐

☐

☐

☐

OTHER TASKS

☐

☐

☐

☐

☐

☐

☐

☐

190

Every child is an artist. The problem is staying an artist when you grow up.
PABLO PICASSO

191

DATE

PRIORITIES

☐ 1. _____

_____

☐ 2. _____

_____

☐ 3. _____

_____

PERSONAL

☐ _____

☐ _____

☐ _____

☐ _____

☐ _____

KEY CALENDAR EVENTS

_____

_____

8 _____

9 _____

10 _____

11 _____

12 _____

1 _____

2 _____

3 _____

4 _____

5 _____

_____

_____

OTHER TASKS

☐ ---

☐ ---

☐ ---

☐ ---

☐ ---

☐ ---

☐ ---

☐ ---

To influence today's culture, we need to have the experience, credentials, and relationships that only come by strategic living.

PHIL COOKE

DATE

KEY CALENDAR EVENTS

PRIORITIES

☐ 1.

☐ 2.

☐ 3.

8

9

10

11

12

1

2

3

4

5

PERSONAL

☐

☐

☐

☐

☐

OTHER TASKS

☐

☐

☐

☐

☐

☐

☐

☐

To make your mark you have to face reality. You can't become a champion surfer practicing in a bathtub.

PHIL COOKE

195

DATE

KEY CALENDAR EVENTS

PRIORITIES

1.

2.

3.

8

9

10

11

12

1

2

3

4

5

PERSONAL

OTHER TASKS

Being unique and different shouldn't mean being fake. Until you value yourself, you won't value your time. Until you value your time, you will not do anything with it.

M. SCOTT PECK

DATE

KEY CALENDAR EVENTS

PRIORITIES

- [ ] 1.
- [ ] 2.
- [ ] 3.

8
9
10
11
12
1
2
3
4
5

PERSONAL

- [ ]
- [ ]
- [ ]
- [ ]
- [ ]

OTHER TASKS

- [ ]
- [ ]
- [ ]
- [ ]
- [ ]
- [ ]
- [ ]
- [ ]

People will sometimes get offended. We should worry about a generation that's been brought up afraid to make choices for fear of offending someone.

PHIL COOKE

199

DATE

KEY CALENDAR EVENTS

PRIORITIES

☐ 1.

☐ 2.

☐ 3.

8

9

10

11

12

1

2

3

4

5

PERSONAL

☐

☐

☐

☐

☐

OTHER TASKS

☐

☐

☐

☐

☐

☐

☐

☐

We are God's masterpiece. He has created us anew in Christ Jesus, so we can do the good things he planned for us long ago.

EPHESIANS 2:10 NLT

DATE

KEY CALENDAR EVENTS

PRIORITIES

☐ 1.

☐ 2.

☐ 3.

8

9

10

11

12

1

2

3

4

5

PERSONAL

☐

☐

☐

☐

☐

OTHER TASKS

☐

☐

☐

☐

☐

☐

☐

☐

What could you be the best in the world at doing? Where could you be remarkable?

PHIL COOKE

DATE

KEY CALENDAR EVENTS

PRIORITIES

- [ ] 1.
- [ ] 2.
- [ ] 3.

8

9

10

11

12

1

2

3

4

5

PERSONAL

- [ ]
- [ ]
- [ ]
- [ ]
- [ ]

OTHER TASKS

- [ ]
- [ ]
- [ ]
- [ ]
- [ ]
- [ ]
- [ ]
- [ ]

We don't make mistakes,
just happy little accidents.
BOB ROSS

DATE

KEY CALENDAR EVENTS

PRIORITIES

- [ ] 1.

- [ ] 2.

- [ ] 3.

8

9

10

11

12

1

2

3

4

5

PERSONAL

- [ ]
- [ ]
- [ ]
- [ ]
- [ ]

OTHER TASKS

- [ ]
- [ ]
- [ ]
- [ ]
- [ ]
- [ ]
- [ ]
- [ ]

What are you here
to accomplish?
PHIL COOKE

DATE

KEY CALENDAR EVENTS

PRIORITIES

☐ 1.

☐ 2.

☐ 3.

8

9

10

11

12

1

2

3

4

5

PERSONAL

☐

☐

☐

☐

☐

OTHER TASKS

☐

☐

☐

☐

☐

☐

☐

☐

What do people think of when they think of you, your product, or your organization?
PHIL COOKE

DATE

PRIORITIES

☐ 1.

☐ 2.

☐ 3.

PERSONAL

☐

☐

☐

☐

☐

KEY CALENDAR EVENTS

8

9

10

11

12

1

2

3

4

5

OTHER TASKS

☐

☐

☐

☐

☐

☐

☐

☐

When the door opens, you'd better be ready to act and have the talent and education to back it up.
Work brings profit, but mere talk leads to poverty!

PROVERBS 14:23 NLT

DATE

KEY CALENDAR EVENTS

PRIORITIES

- [ ] 1.

- [ ] 2.

- [ ] 3.

8

9

10

11

12

1

2

3

4

5

PERSONAL

- [ ]
- [ ]
- [ ]
- [ ]
- [ ]

OTHER TASKS

- [ ]
- [ ]
- [ ]
- [ ]
- [ ]
- [ ]
- [ ]
- [ ]

What specific and personal reason drives you to do what you aspire to?

PHIL COOKE

DATE

KEY CALENDAR EVENTS

PRIORITIES

☐ 1.

☐ 2.

☐ 3.

8

9

10

11

12

1

2

3

4

5

PERSONAL

☐

☐

☐

☐

☐

OTHER TASKS

☐

☐

☐

☐

☐

☐

☐

☐

I am not afraid...
I was born to do this.
JOAN OF ARC

215

DATE

KEY CALENDAR EVENTS

PRIORITIES

☐ 1.

☐ 2.

☐ 3.

8

9

10

11

12

1

2

3

4

5

PERSONAL

☐

☐

☐

☐

☐

OTHER TASKS

☐

☐

☐

☐

☐

☐

☐

☐

What's your motivation: traumas or triumphs? Building your brand story often begins with your past and your purpose.

PHIL COOKE

DATE

KEY CALENDAR EVENTS

PRIORITIES

- [ ] 1.
- [ ] 2.
- [ ] 3.

8
9
10
11
12
1
2
3
4
5

PERSONAL

- [ ]
- [ ]
- [ ]
- [ ]
- [ ]

OTHER TASKS

- [ ]
- [ ]
- [ ]
- [ ]
- [ ]
- [ ]
- [ ]
- [ ]

We must have perseverance and above all, confidence in ourselves. We must believe that we are gifted for something, and that this thing must be attained.

MARIE CURIE

DATE

KEY CALENDAR EVENTS

PRIORITIES

☐ 1.

☐ 2.

☐ 3.

8

9

10

11

12

1

2

3

4

5

PERSONAL

☐

☐

☐

☐

☐

OTHER TASKS

☐

☐

☐

☐

☐

☐

☐

☐

When it comes to others, be gracious. But when it comes to yourself, be ruthless. Be ruthless about your commitments. Be ruthless about your intellectual growth. Be ruthless about finishing well.

PHIL COOKE

DATE

KEY CALENDAR EVENTS

PRIORITIES

☐ 1.

☐ 2.

☐ 3.

8

9

10

11

12

1

2

3

4

5

PERSONAL

☐

☐

☐

☐

☐

OTHER TASKS

☐

☐

☐

☐

☐

☐

☐

☐

When we discover our purpose, values are what help us make the right decisions regarding it.

PHIL COOKE

223

DATE

KEY CALENDAR EVENTS

PRIORITIES

☐ 1.

☐ 2.

☐ 3.

8

9

10

11

12

1

2

3

4

5

PERSONAL

☐

☐

☐

☐

☐

OTHER TASKS

☐

☐

☐

☐

☐

☐

☐

☐

To invent, you need a good imagination and a pile of junk.
THOMAS EDISON

DATE

KEY CALENDAR EVENTS

PRIORITIES

☐ 1.

☐ 2.

☐ 3.

8

9

10

11

12

1

2

3

4

5

PERSONAL

☐

☐

☐

☐

☐

OTHER TASKS

☐

☐

☐

☐

☐

☐

☐

☐

Who do you want
to influence?

PHIL COOKE

DATE

KEY CALENDAR EVENTS

PRIORITIES

☐ 1.

☐ 2.

☐ 3.

8

9

10

11

12

1

2

3

4

5

PERSONAL

☐

☐

☐

☐

☐

OTHER TASKS

☐

☐

☐

☐

☐

☐

☐

☐

You can design and create and build the most wonderful place in the world. But it takes people to make the dream a reality.

WALT DISNEY

229

DATE

KEY CALENDAR EVENTS

PRIORITIES

1.

2.

3.

8

9

10

11

12

1

2

3

4

5

PERSONAL

OTHER TASKS

You can overcome any obstacle as long as you know your destination.
PHIL COOKE

DATE

KEY CALENDAR EVENTS

PRIORITIES

- [ ] 1.

- [ ] 2.

- [ ] 3.

8

9

10

11

12

1

2

3

4

5

PERSONAL

- [ ]
- [ ]
- [ ]
- [ ]
- [ ]

OTHER TASKS

- [ ]
- [ ]
- [ ]
- [ ]
- [ ]
- [ ]
- [ ]
- [ ]

Who's painting the portrait of your life?
PHIL COOKE

233

DATE

KEY CALENDAR EVENTS

PRIORITIES

- [ ] 1.
- [ ] 2.
- [ ] 3.

8
9
10
11
12
1
2
3
4
5

PERSONAL

- [ ]
- [ ]
- [ ]
- [ ]
- [ ]

OTHER TASKS

- [ ]
- [ ]
- [ ]
- [ ]
- [ ]
- [ ]
- [ ]
- [ ]

Wisdom and money can get you almost anything, but only wisdom can save your life.

ECCLESIASTES 7:12 NLT

235

DATE

KEY CALENDAR EVENTS

PRIORITIES

☐ 1.

☐ 2.

☐ 3.

8

9

10

11

12

1

2

3

4

5

PERSONAL

☐

☐

☐

☐

☐

OTHER TASKS

☐

☐

☐

☐

☐

☐

☐

☐

Writing my blog has saved me thousands on therapy.

PHIL COOKE

DATE

KEY CALENDAR EVENTS

PRIORITIES

☐ 1.

☐ 2.

☐ 3.

PERSONAL

☐

☐

☐

☐

☐

8

9

10

11

12

1

2

3

4

5

OTHER TASKS

☐

☐

☐

☐

☐

☐

☐

☐

You'll never stumble upon the unexpected if you stick only to the familiar.

ED CATMULL

DATE

KEY CALENDAR EVENTS

PRIORITIES

- [ ] 1.
- [ ] 2.
- [ ] 3.

8
9
10
11
12
1
2
3
4
5

PERSONAL

- [ ]
- [ ]
- [ ]
- [ ]
- [ ]

OTHER TASKS

- [ ]
- [ ]
- [ ]
- [ ]
- [ ]
- [ ]
- [ ]
- [ ]

You can't change what happened, but you can change what happens next.
PHIL COOKE

DATE

KEY CALENDAR EVENTS

PRIORITIES

☐ 1.

☐ 2.

☐ 3.

8

9

10

11

12

1

2

3

4

5

PERSONAL

☐

☐

☐

☐

☐

OTHER TASKS

☐

☐

☐

☐

☐

☐

☐

☐

You have brains in your head.
You have feet in your shoes.
You can steer yourself in any
direction you choose.
DR. SEUSS

DATE

KEY CALENDAR EVENTS

PRIORITIES

☐ 1.

☐ 2.

☐ 3.

8

9

10

11

12

1

2

3

4

5

PERSONAL

☐

☐

☐

☐

☐

OTHER TASKS

☐

☐

☐

☐

☐

☐

☐

☐

Your power to choose is remarkable.
The ability to change your life is
directly connected to your ability to
make choices and take responsibility
for those choices.

PHIL COOKE

245

DATE

KEY CALENDAR EVENTS

PRIORITIES

☐ 1.

☐ 2.

☐ 3.

8

9

10

11

12

1

2

3

4

5

PERSONAL

☐

☐

☐

☐

☐

OTHER TASKS

☐

☐

☐

☐

☐

☐

☐

☐

246

God saw everything that he had made, and behold, it was very good.
GENESIS 1:31 ESV

DATE

KEY CALENDAR EVENTS

PRIORITIES

☐ 1.

☐ 2.

☐ 3.

8

9

10

11

12

1

2

3

4

5

PERSONAL

☐

☐

☐

☐

☐

OTHER TASKS

☐

☐

☐

☐

☐

☐

☐

☐

How are you connecting with people to get your ideas heard? You've got to cut through today's distracted culture and get on their radar.

PHIL COOKE

INDEX

INDEX

INDEX

INDEX

ABOUT PHIL COOKE

An internationally known filmmaker, writer, and media consultant, Phil Cooke has produced media programming in more than 60 countries and created many of the most influential and successful Christian and inspirational TV programs in history. Phil's book *One Big Thing: Discovering What you Were Born to Do* will help you find the great purpose for your life. His book *Unique: Telling Your Story in the Age of Brands and Social Media* is changing the way nonprofit and religious organizations engage today's culture with a message of hope. His new book *The Way Back: How Christians Blew Our Credibility and How We Get it Back* challenges Christians to confront the real reasons our faith is losing influence.

Joel Osteen calls Phil "one of the most innovative communicators of our generation."

Ralph Winter, producer of *X-Men, Wolverine*, and *Planet of the Apes*, says, "I guarantee Phil Cooke will transform your thinking about using the media in the twenty-first century."

Phil has written for The Huffington Post, Fast Company, Forbes.com, Wired.com, and FoxNews.com. Download a free eBook on creativity at Phil's website: philcooke.com. Follow Phil on Twitter and Instagram @PhilCooke.